P9-DFZ-081

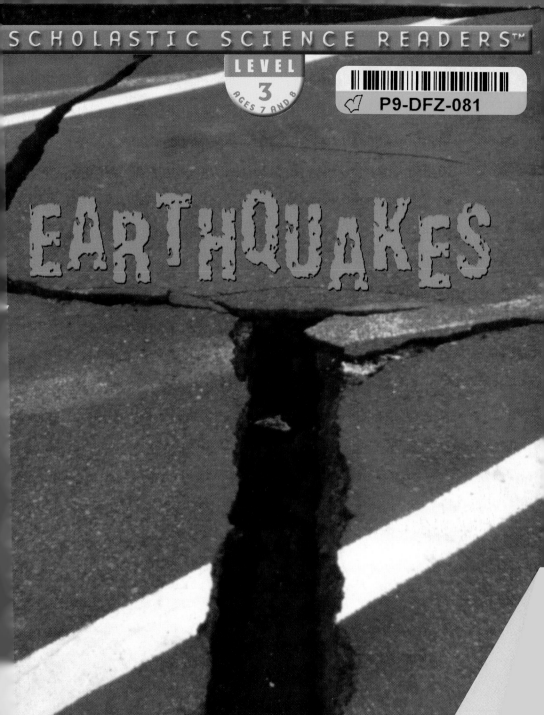

EARTHQUAKES

Deborah Heiligman

SCHOLASTIC
REFERENCE

Photo credits: Cover: Deborah Davis/Getty Images, Inc.
Page 1: Michael S. Yamashita/Corbis; 3, 4: Roger Ressmeyer/Corbis;
5: Lois Bernstein/Wide World Photos; 6: Owen Franken/Corbis;
7: David Young-Wolff/PhotoEdit; 9: J. D. Griggs/Hawaii Volcano Observatory/United States
Geological Survey; 10: Mehau Kulyk/Scieence Photo Library/ Photo Researchers, Inc.;
11: Sarah Longacre; 12: Science Photo Library/Photo Researchers, Inc.; 13: R. E.
Wallace/USGS; 14: David Young-Wolff/PhotoEdit; 15: Reuters/Robert Sorbo/Archive Photos;
17: David & Peter Turnley/Corbis; 18: Vince Streano/Corbis; 19: Russell D. Curtis/Photo
Researchers, Inc.; 20: North Wind Pictures; 21: N. Carter/North Wind Pictures;
22: Bettmann/Corbis; 23: Bettmann/Corbis; 24: Corbis; 25: Corbis; 26: Otto Greule
Jr./Allsport USA; 27: E. V. Levendecker/USGS; 28: Bettmann/Corbis; 29, 31 (top and bottom),
33, 34: Roger Ressmeyer/Corbis; 35: National Aeronautics and Space Administration/Science
Photo Library/Photo Researchers, Inc.; 36: Ellen M. Banner © The Seattle Times;
37: Roger Ressmeyer/Corbis; 38: Eric Draper/AP/Wide World Photos;
39: Roger Ressmeyer/Corbis; 41: Reuters/Eriko Sugita/Archive Photos;
43: Enric Marti/Associated Press; 45: Clark Mishler/Corbis.

An earthquake is always a surprise.

All of a sudden, without any warning, the ground begins to move. It shakes. It bumps. It rolls. Sometimes it feels as if the ground beneath you has become water.

In a powerful earthquake, there is a loud, rumbling noise.

You might think it's a large truck or train going by.

Then, before you can figure out what's happening, bookcases topple over, dishes and glasses crash onto the floor, windows and television screens pop out.

The wood in your house creaks and moans.

A young girl left homeless by a powerful earthquake in Kobe, Japan, in 1995, clings to her pet dog.

Cats dash outside. Streetlights sway, car alarms go off, dogs bark up and down the streets.

The power may go out.

In very strong earthquakes, roofs can cave in, buildings tumble, bridges fall down, and roadways collapse.

Rescue operations continued for days after a major earthquake in Mexico City in 1985.

Then, as suddenly as it began, it is over. Earthquakes don't last very long—from a few seconds to a few minutes. A lot happens in that short time. An earthquake can be the most powerful—and dangerous—force in nature.

But not all earthquakes cause damage. We can't even feel most of the earthquakes that occur. There are more than 8,000 minor earthquakes every day on our planet. But less than 100 are strong enough for us to feel. And of those, only a very few cause damage.

Minor earthquakes happen every day, but we don't feel them.

Why are there so many earthquakes? You might think that the earth we walk on and build our houses on is stable, solid, and still. But it's not. The ground beneath us is moving all the time!

At the very center of the earth is a solid inner core. Around that core is the outer core, which is made up of very, very hot, moving liquid. Sitting on top of that is the earth's mantle, which is made of rock. Some of the mantle is very hot, and it moves very slowly, like chocolate pudding when you pour it out of a pot.

The movement of the mantle also causes volcanoe to erupt. In this photo, lava flows from Hawaii Kilauea volcano into the Pacific Ocear

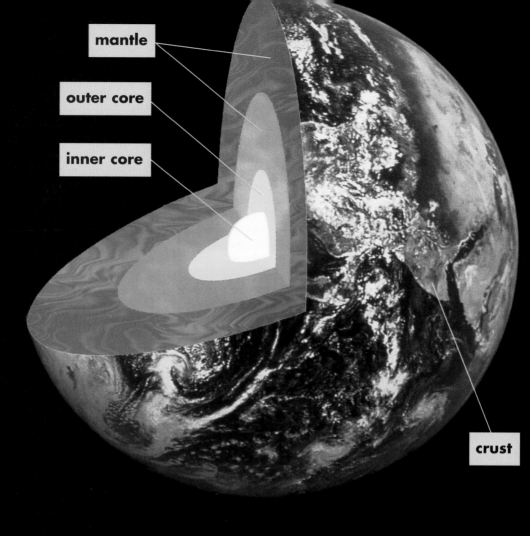

mantle

outer core

inner core

crust

Above the mantle is the earth's crust, the part we walk on and build our houses on. The movement of the mantle has caused the earth's crust to crack in many places.

Picture the shell of a hard-boiled egg. When you knock the egg against a hard surface, the shell cracks into pieces. But the egg still keeps its shape.

Earth's crust looks like that. It is cracked, but still holds its round shape.

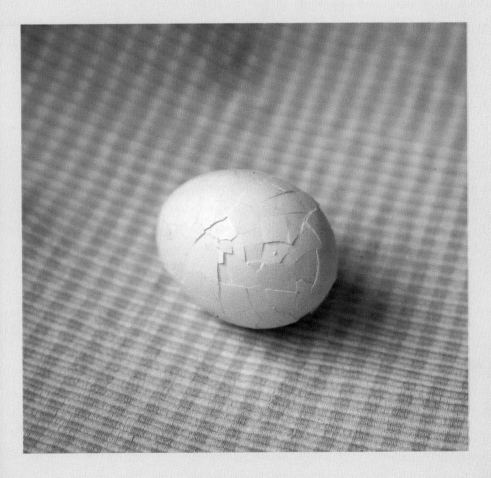

Pieces of the earth's crust are called **tectonic** (tek-**tahn**-ik) **plates**. These plates are constantly moving, because the mantle below them is moving. Sometimes, two plates will get stuck along what is called a **fault**. The plates push and push along the fault until the stress is so great that some of the rock slips, cracks, breaks, or buckles. That's what causes an earthquake.

This artwork shows the outlines of Earth's main tectonic plates in red.

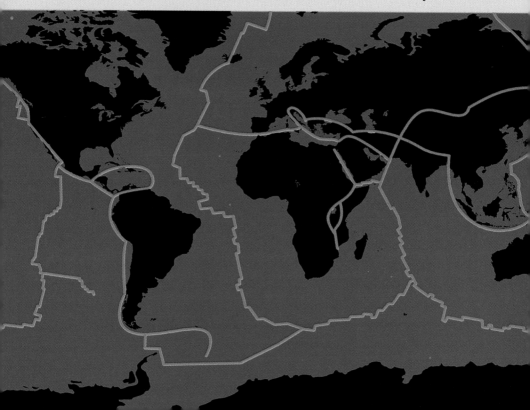

California's San Andreas Fault

Most faults are under the surface of the earth and you can't see them. But you can see one in California. The San Andreas Fault is about 600 miles (970 kilometers) long. The earth along the fault moves all the time. It moves gradually, about 2 inches (5 centimeters) a year. There have been many earthquakes along this fault. Places like this, where plates move along faults, are called **earthquake zones**.

Here's a way to understand how earthquakes happen. Try snapping your fingers. You push and push and push your fingers together and sideways. Finally your fingers move suddenly and you snap. That's what happens in an earthquake. When the rock slips and breaks, this snap sends shock waves throughout the earth.

A powerful earthquake shook the Seattle, Washington, area for 45 seconds on February 28, 2001.

These waves cause vibrations in the earth. Sometimes the vibration is no more than that caused by a truck passing by, or a subway. Sometimes the vibration is a lot stronger. There have been earthquakes that were even stronger than an atomic bomb. But earthquakes this strong are quite rare.

The place where the rock first breaks under the surface of the earth is called the **focus** (**foh**-kuhs). The point on the surface of the earth right above the focus is called the **epicenter** (**ep**-i-*sen*-tuhr) of the quake. This is where we feel the strongest shaking.

After a big earthquake there are usually many **aftershocks**. An aftershock is also an earthquake. It is usually not as strong as the first quake, but it can be quite powerful. Sometimes there is more than one aftershock. Aftershocks can happen the next day, the next week, or even a month or a year later.

A boy stands outside a ruined apartment building followin a devastating earthquake in Armenia in 1988. Aftershoc can make survivors fearful of returning to their home

A scientist checks seismograph readings.

Scientists use special instruments called **seismographs** (**size**-muh-*grafs*) to measure the strength of an earthquake. They rate earthquakes on a scale. The higher the number, the stronger the quake.

A large earthquake might have a **magnitude** (**mag**-nuh-*tood*) of 6.5 or 7 or even higher. The smaller ones have magnitudes of 2 or 3.

Take a Closer Look

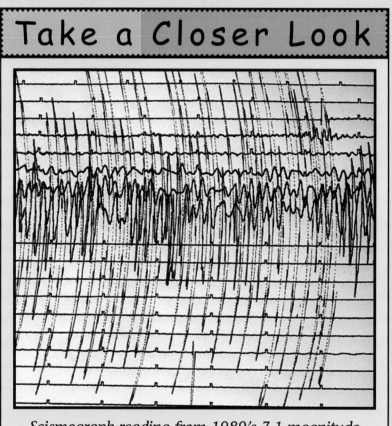

Seismograph reading from 1989's 7.1 magnitude earthquake near Loma Prieta Peak, in California

A woodcut shows the damage that followed the New Madrid earthquake.

One of the strongest earthquakes to hit the United States was in Missouri in 1811. There was actually a series of quakes, or one big quake and its aftershocks, in and around the town of New Madrid. The first quake was in December of 1811, and the last in February 1812.

These quakes were felt 1,000 miles (1,609 kilometers) away. The seismograph hadn't been invented yet, but if it had, scientists think the largest of the quakes would have measured 8 or more. The quakes were so powerful they changed the course of the Mississippi River.

Bald eagles nest above Reelfoot Lake, which was created when the New Madrid earthquake changed the course of the Mississippi River.

Houses slid into cracks in the earth during the Good Friday earthquake in Anchorage, Alaska, in 1964.

There also have been strong earthquakes in Alaska, Greece, Turkey, Japan, Mexico, and all over the world. But the earthquakes that cause the most damage are usually those that strike cities. In cities, a lot of people live close together in buildings that can topple.

One of the most famous is the earthquake that struck in the early morning of April 18, 1906, in San Francisco, California. It had a magnitude of 8.25.

San Francisco, 1906

The quake lasted only about 40 seconds, but it seriously damaged San Francisco. Houses and buildings tumbled down. Gas lines broke, setting off fires that raged for three days.

San Francisco, 1906

San Francisco, 1906

Most of the city, primarily structures built of wood, burned down. About 28,000 buildings were destroyed and close to 3,000 people died.

An earthquake in 1989 caused girders on the Oakland Bay Bridge to shift.

Eighty-three years later, in 1989, another strong earthquake hit San Francisco just as the third game of the World Series was about to begin.

The Series was a dream for the San Francisco area—it was between the San Francisco Giants and their neighbors, the Oakland A's. But everyone had to leave Candlestick Park and the World Series was postponed.

A young fan shows his disappointment after an earthquake stopped the World Series in 1989.

San Francisco, 1989

Again, fires raged. The San Francisco
fire department had to fight thirty-four
large fires at once! This wasn't easy,
because the water lines under the ground
broke, so the firefighters could not pump
water from fire hydrants. They had to
use fireboats to pump water from San
Francisco Bay.

Fortunately, almost a century later, many of the buildings in San Francisco were sturdier than those standing in 1906. And because people knew how to be safe in an earthquake, and how to help others, fewer lives were lost. Still, more than $6 billion worth of damage was done.

San Francisco, 1989

Scientists say that it's not earthquakes that kill people; it's falling buildings that do. That's why all over the world, especially in earthquake zones, engineers and architects try to make old buildings safer.

And when they build new buildings, especially skyscrapers, they make them so that they sway, but don't fall, when earthquakes hit.

A scientist performs a safety test on a small model house to learn more about earthquake damage and how to prevent it.

Builders use stronger materials, and materials that are flexible, like rubber and steel. Some buildings are on rollers. Others have steel beams anchored into the ground.

Scientists are trying to invent new ways to make buildings safer. One idea is to put a heavy weight inside a building. The weight is set up so that if the building moves in one direction, the weight moves in the opposite direction. This may help to keep the building from falling.

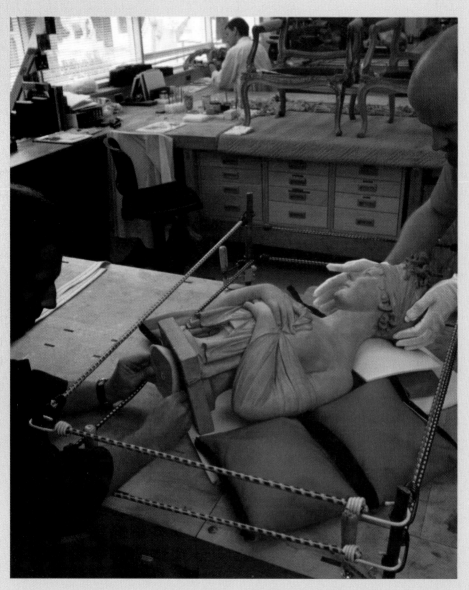

Just as rollers beneath buildings can lessen earthquake damage, art museums often install special bases to prevent statues from falling and breaking during earthquakes.

Another way to save lives is to predict when earthquakes will occur, so people can get to safety. So far, scientists can tell which areas of the world are more likely to have earthquakes, but they can't predict exactly when and where an earthquake will occur.

These scientists have dug a trench so they can study soil layers, searching for evidence of faults.

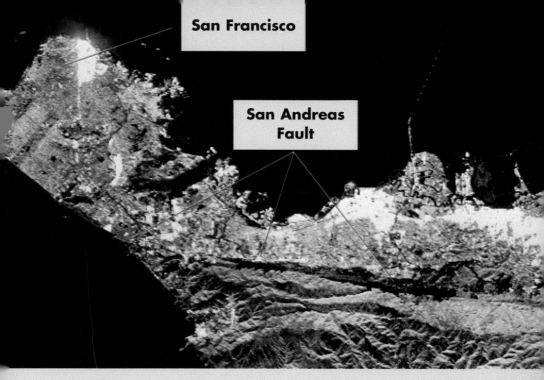

San Francisco

San Andreas
Fault

*This radar image of San Francisco and the San Andreas Fault
was taken during a space shuttle mission in 1994.*

But scientists are working on it! Using satellites, they watch the earth's plates move from space. The plates move very slowly—about the speed our fingernails grow. The satellites' vision is so sharp, the pictures show even the smallest movements. By studying these pictures, scientists might be able to predict the next "big one."

Scientists also set off explosions beneath the ground to imitate small earthquakes. Then they watch to see what happens. From these explosions, scientists learn what to expect during a real earthquake.

When the Seattle Kingdome was brought down with explosives, to make room for a new stadium, scientists in the area paid special attention. They studied the vibrations from the explosion, hoping to learn more about how vibrations from earthquakes travel.

Soil layers can also provide clues to earthquakes that took place in the past.

Geologists can also tell, by studying soil, if there were earthquakes in certain areas long, long ago.

First-grade students in Los Angeles, California, learn to take cover during an earthquake drill.

Although earthquakes can happen anywhere, they are most likely to happen in earthquake zones. So people in earthquake zones have to be prepared. They bolt down heavy furniture and bookcases. Schools and families have earthquake drills. Kids learn to move away from windows and heavy objects that might fall. They practice getting under a heavy table, bed, or counter. Outside, they practice getting away from buildings, trees, and power lines.

Families have earthquake kits at home and children take small earthquake kits to school. The kits include water, food in cans and boxes, flashlights, a battery-powered radio, space blankets, and a favorite toy or book.

A family practices an earthquake evacuation.

In Japan, once a year, on the anniversary of a big quake, the whole city of Tokyo holds an enormous earthquake drill. Everyone pretends there is an earthquake.

Children climb into a machine that creates earthquake-like conditions. People practice putting out fires and getting to safety. Rescue squads practice with their tools and equipment.

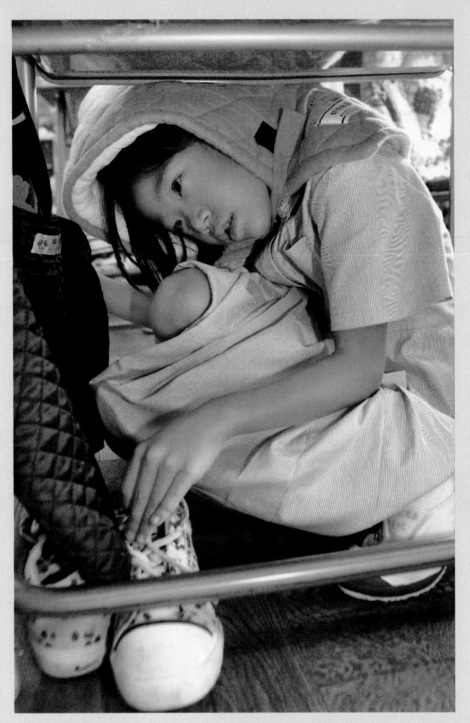

Earthquake drills take place in Japan every September, on the anniversary of the Great Kanto Earthquake of 1923.

After a real earthquake, people help one another. They try to rescue those who are trapped in buildings. Specially-trained rescue dogs sometimes help. The dogs pick up the scent of humans and follow their noses to find people trapped in collapsed buildings.

After an earthquake, people also give one another food, water, and places to sleep. They fix up houses and schools.

They talk about where they were when the earth shook. Talking about what they've been through helps many people to feel better.

*Dutch rescue workers used dogs to search for survivors
after an earthquake in Turkey in 1999.*

And sometimes they remind each other that earthquakes aren't always bad.

Scientists have learned almost everything they know about the inside of the earth from studying the vibrations of earthquakes.

They also know that ancient earthquakes reshaped the earth and created many of our mountains, rivers, and landscapes. The forces that can destroy have also made our planet a beautiful place to live.

The harbor at Anchorage, Alaska, is surrounded by a backdrop o
mountains. Earthquake activity has brought both dramat.
scenery and serious damage to the Anchorage are

Glossary

aftershock—an earthquake after the main earthquake; the aftershock is less powerful

earthquake zones—areas of the earth where earthquakes are most likely to happen due to the movement of tectonic plates

epicenter (**ep**-i-*sen*-tuhr)—the place on the earth's surface that is directly above the focus, the point where an earthquake begins

fault—a break in the earth's crust where large masses of rock often slide past each other

focus (**foh**-kuhs)—the spot under the surface of the earth where the rock first breaks, thus starting an earthquake

magnitude (**mag**-nuh-*tood*)—the measure of the strength and power of an earthquake

seismographs (**size**-muh-*grafs*)—instruments that measure the movements of the earth

tectonic (tek-**tahn**-ik) **plates**—the approximately 30 pieces that the earth's crust is broken into. The tectonic plates are always moving, very slowly.

Index

A Note to Parents

Learning to read is such an exciting time in a child's life. You may delight in sharing your favorite fairy tales and picture books with your child.

But don't forget the importance of introducing your child to the world of nonfiction. The ability to read and comprehend factual material will be essential to your child in school, and throughout life. The Scholastic Science Readers™ series was created especially with beginning readers in mind. These books, with their clear texts and beautiful photographs, will help you to share the wonders of science with *your* new reader.

Suggested Activity

Now that you've learned about earthquakes, think about what you can do to help to make your family earthquake-aware!

Has an earthquake ever happened in the city or town where you live? Ask your parents or guardians to go with you to the library to find out.

Make a list of things you would need if an earthquake were to happen, and work with your family to prepare an earthquake kit. Make sure everyone knows where the kit will be. Talk to your family about what to do just in case an earthquake should happen, whether you are inside or outside, at home or at school.